Gathering Wholeness
The Art of Identifying and Exploring Parts of Self

Cat Caracelo M.A.

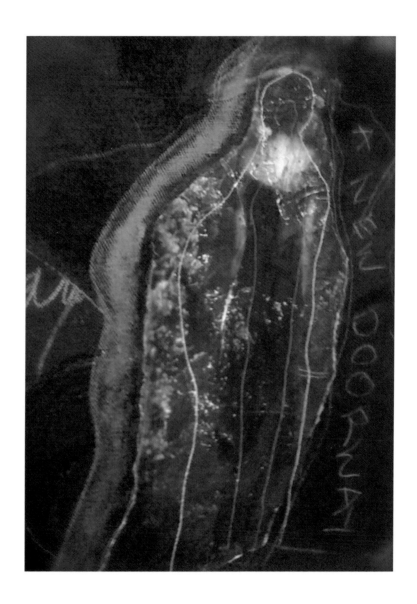

I dedicate this book to my known and unknown family.

I honor my parents, they were my original teachers and encouraged me to follow my inner compass.

Thank you to my husband Danny, for your constant love, bringing lightness and laughter into my life and forever picking up the bits and pieces I tend to scatter behind me as I create.

To my three children, Sacha, Darcy and Jake, we circle each other with deep abiding love and I am grateful for your endless support.

To the sister of my heart, my friends and the many women who journey with me, you are a constant source of inspiration and joy.

May we continue to seek, find and thrive in our wholeness.

Table of Contents

Introduction

Gathering Wholeness offers a series of psycho-spiritual, theoretical and highly practical ideas that will open you to new integrative methods for exploring, identifying and working with parts of self. This work is a call to explore and create with patterns that we experience in, and throughout, our lifetime. This is depth work and its purpose is to make space to dip in and dive down, landing within our own vast pool of inner knowledge. Finding ways, through art and process based inquiry, to work with parts of self, life stage transitions, shadow material and healing arts, creating identifiable pathways to support extended personal exploration and growth. As humans, we are called to explore, to experience, to heal and activate our energies within this life. Gathering Wholeness is designed to be both a personal reference and source of information. It is full of touchstones. My hope is that it will connect you to your own place of entering.

Art is here taken to mean knowledge realized in action.
- Rene Daumal

My own life path has informed my work. I have, like you, experienced periods of challenge, some causing me years of pain and confusion. Because of the transformation I have experienced working with parts of self and other dynamic models I share in this workbook, these challenges and wounds have become my greatest sources of exploration and inspiration. As an artist, I explore the personal and collective inner landscape and psyche through my own mixed media art, incorporating visual narrative, archetype, symbol and a layered form that I call *Mythos Journey*. I often create from topics of hidden and disowned emotions. I follow my dreams, desires and clues, unraveling and reweaving my lived and intuited experiences to find new perspectives. I recognize the tremendous potential for healing found in exploring, exposing and embracing the shadow, as well as expanding my understanding of spectrum of self. These are accomplished through art and living. I am passionate about creating communities and circles that inspire both individual and collective healing and wholeness.

I offer Gathering Wholeness as a means to discover and explore more deeply some of these techniques and theories in easy and accessible ways. This art and life workbook is also a structural support for expanding your "language" opening to exploration and activation for your inner work.

1 | The Edge

Call out to the edge,
beyond the edge,
where the ancestors
and elders wait for you
to remember them again.

Call out to the edge,
beyond the edge,
to ask for the power
to be passed to you
like a sacred flame.

Call out to the edge,
beyond the edge,
where the sleepers lie
waiting for your voice to rise
from deep inside,
to ring out,
banish fear,
rouse them from their
ancient dreamtime.

Call out to the edge,
beyond the edge,
to ask them for your
lost treasures
to be returned to you.
Passed like a torch.

Call out and claim again
that which is yours:
Creative Fire.
Visionary Passion.
Healing Magic.
Deep Connection.

Call out to the edge,
beyond the edge,
to those who
have carried these
gifts before you,
so that they may
guide you, once again.

Myth linking myth,
Call out to the edge,
beyond the edge.
Re-remember your whole self,
gather your dismembered
parts back together,
healing old wounds
that flow through
the rivers of time.

You are the
one and the many
walking the path of discovery
and destiny.

- Cat Caracelo

We all have an edge, even another that is beyond the precipice we can sense is there. This is often the place of pain and fear. This is the abyss, the place of unknown outcomes.

We humans do not like the edge; most of us do not even want to know that there might be another edge beyond the ones we see. Everything in us says, "Back up, stay safe, don't go near it or you might fall."

What we don't remember is that the edge holds a kind of clarity, giving us the ability to see far. The edge holds principles of possibility, understanding and capacity building. When we find ways to develop courage and find guidance, calling out to the edge becomes an adventure, a quest or journey. The edge is also the place of entering into transformation; it is a place of opportunity and active visioning.

The abyss of the unknown does not have to mean a long hard fall, it might mean releasing, letting go, and dipping into the wind to find your wings.

"Traveling from the known to the unknown requires crossing an abyss of emptiness.

We first experience disorientation and confusion. Then, if we are willing to cross the abyss in curious and playful wonder, we enter an expansive and untamed country that has its own rhythm. Time melts and thoughts become stories, music, poems, images, ideas.

This is the intelligence of the heart, but by that I don't just mean emotions. I mean a vast range of receptive and connective abilities: intuition, innovation, wisdom, creativity, sensitivity....and meaning."
- Dawna Markova

The call to the edge guided me in real ways, through a process of inquiry and journeying into my life; I was able to gather and integrate parts of myself that were lost and disowned. I found other parts of self that were completely unexpressed. Over the years I have developed my own language of journeying and now guide women worldwide as they navigate their own depth process.

In my years of training, my mentor and teacher Debbie Ford would often share with me, "We humans are meaning making machines." For some time I did not fully grasp this truth. I was still in the grip of my meaning making, focusing on the details of my wounded life I was mid fall down the rabbit hole. Locked in single threaded perspectives my stories seemed to help me orient myself. In fact, they kept me in free fall. My meaning making made me feel safe but my edge brought me into relationship with my own vision of landing.

My edge was pain and lostness.

I was calling out beyond that pain. During these years, as I traveled my own healing path, I developed a coaching practice integrating depth process, mindfulness techniques, emotional literacy, adult learning styles, transformative practices and expressive arts. My previous work and life experiences with wellness, education and mental health support informed my own discovery process.

Guidance from other powerful teachers, shamanic practitioners, healing artists and visionary dreamers also informed my work. My depth work incorporated Psychosynthesis, more commonly known as Parts of Self work, from the very beginning and was present for years before I knew what it was offering me.

Reclaiming art as a personal language met me around the time that my life was falling apart. I had lost track of myself over the years of living, struggling through a complex marriage, landing in work I did not love, raising children, one whom had a life threatening illness, loving and supporting others. I had inadvertently poured my own life energy out.

I was awakened by a serious back injury that required a long wait for surgery.
I was awakened to my own disintegration.
I realized I could not sustain the way I had been living my life. I turned to introspective silence and made space for listening. For the next year I was in a cocoon, tending to others as I could, all the while trying to gather my own pieces back together, to find some answers. It was at this time I returned to a degree program and mutually ended a twenty-two year marriage.

As I marked my new path, engaging in profound personal process, I found that art-making informed me in unexpected and illuminating ways. Serving as a symbolic language that brought me back to my own roots, I began to find the answers that I was seeking.

As I was gathering my pieces and parts, delving into studies and creating the life-work that I love, my creative process guided me to inner wisdom and a base of knowledge that had been hidden. Art became the language of my soul but it took me many more years to fully claim my artist self.

Prompts

What is your edge?

_____

_____

_____

_____

_____

_____

_____

How are you holding fear, grief and pain?

_____

_____

_____

_____

_____

_____

_____

_____

_____

_____

What is the sensation of being on the edge?

_____

_____

_____

_____

_____

_____

_____

What is stuck? What are you reclaiming?

_____

_____

_____

_____

_____

_____

_____

_____

_____

Creative Mapping & Musing

Gathering Wholeness

2 | The Call to Wholeness

Wholeness is a big idea.

The call to wholeness is a happening not just a topic.

This book is based in an experiential approach to ideas, translating them through art and life, exploring the details that are unique to us. Seeking and finding our own points of resonance and intersection help us to become self-referring as we return to wholeness.

The call to wholeness is subtle and often unsettling, it can be easily ignored. When one becomes attuned, the call invites us to step into the unknown. The call is sparked by noticing, calling our attention inward. The attunement process can develop slowly or become amplified through conscious connecting.

The call to wholeness is something that you will feel deep inside. In the beginning, the call is often heard as a deep sorrow. At life stage transitions, or unexpected threshold moments, the call to wholeness may come through fear, grief or pain.

For many the call is unwinding the source of deep confusion and disorientation, a subtle greyness that permeates life like a fog.

The call comes from our deep psyche.

The call comes when we are ready to know more than we have known before.

The call comes when we are ready to engage healing and expand our own expression.

The Many Paths to Wholeness

The call is about energizing and developing the expression of the whole self in new ways. There are many paths to gathering wholeness. There are many means of entering, engaging and exploring who we are at any given time. The nature of expanding capacity honors each of these ways. This work is energetic, it brings back into focus our own abilities, strengths, vision and possibilities.

Wholeness is a self-defined, initiatory process of becoming fully expressed. I would not assume or presume to identify <u>your</u> path to wholeness. That is yours to work with, and although you may seek support and guidance, it is your journey alone. This way of connecting into transformative process, as a form, is considered depth work because it involves unraveling our own parts, aspects, expressions and experiences back to their source, not only diving deep to follow our story threads but reweaving them into more solid and clear form. It is also a movement-based concept, it is not an arrival-based absolute.

I am whole and now complete is an example of a concrete reflection.

I am whole, evermore learning and growing is an example of an open concept.

Many of us engage in healing to activate our energies in the direction of wellness or to release the residue of unconscious beliefs, core wounds and victimization that has been held.

I am too big, too loud and too much is an example of a concrete reflection.

I am healing my too big, too loud and too much stories and experiences is an example of an open reflection.

One statement is not more or less true, they are simply personal explorations in perspective. They are similar expressions of lived experience offering varied viewpoints that are held in the body as energy. For anyone who has experienced deep trauma you will recognize that this is a very difficult energy to harness, shift and embody. By nature, victimization and trauma is triggering. There can be long established inner strategies to remain safe. These can be challenging patterns to work with yet they are also the very ones that call us to wholeness.

What I know is that healing is not the same as curing or eradicating. Healing and wholeness take into account our circumstances such as, health, mobility, stamina, strengths, weaknesses, needs, wants and desires. These can be explored in ways that meet your needs through image, paint, mixed media, dialoguing, journaling or poetry.

Art is an act of the soul, not the intellect…we are in the realm of the sacred. We are involved with forces and energies larger than our own. We are engaged in a sacred transaction of which we know only a little: the shadow, not the shape.

- Julia Cameron

Embracing the whole self is active and it can take some time to awaken to the call. Even more time may be spent as we come to understand the call's purpose and begin to respond.

Being called by one's inner self, toward a more fully expressed whole self, is aligned with the developmental process of individuation and integration. Some refer to this concept as the higher self, considering the energetics of one's own life force or vibration.

Consider the rising energy of an evolutionary self, a complex multi-faceted expression of the whole self, growing in spirals and cycles of integration and disintegration, while activating developmental phases of healing and wholeness.

However you identify this process for yourself you will recognize it internally. When you hear the call you will know. Sacred listening and inner attention is the first response of answering a call.

Listening is active and embodied, a sensory pathway to one's own inner and imaginal landscape. Responding to a call is always, initially, an inside job. Over time, the process of listening and connecting leads to discovery; at that time the inner expression can start to become externalized.

The core self, essence or soul as one's singular identity, has been approached over thousands of years through research, medicine, science, philosophy, theory, theology and practice. My approach is an integration of information connecting theory and research to wisdom that resides within, exploring the multiple selves rather than the singular. This reflection of the whole self with many parts, elements, and aspects is indeed singularly ours; answering the call to journey with wholeness and discovering our own shadows and shapes.

Prompts

What is rising energy that you can identify?

_____

_____

_____

_____

_____

_____

_____

Where are you on your path to wholeness?

_____

_____

_____

_____

_____

_____

_____

What is calling to you?

_____

_____

_____

_____

_____

_____

_____

_____

_____

_____

Creative Mapping & Musing

Gathering Wholeness

3 | Exploring Parts of Self

Using the lenses of psycho-spiritual theories, including developmental, psychological, and spiritual models, within experiential inquiry helps us to develop an understanding of our many parts of self.

We are complex multi-faceted human beings. We have attributes, elements and aspects of self that are different, powerful and paradoxical. We are more than a single self, or singular identity. We are dynamic.

Looking through the lenses of our many parts, rather than our single self, invites insights to grow and expand. The value of engaging this process is based on activating personal insight and experimenting. The experiential process relies on mystery and the willingness to be with the unknown. This approach to identifying and working with parts of self, or subpersonalities as they are formally called, are accessed and expressed in many ways, often through creative process.

Remember the old adage, Less is More?

In my work, More is More.

Using techniques of depth coaching, journey process, transformative art, healing and consciousness practices has shown me the value of knowing who I am.

Wholeness can only happen with understanding. We cannot understand what we do not see. All depth process requires a commitment to seeking, to deepening one's own relationship with the many inner selves, stories, experiences and intuited connections.

This work may require opening locked doors, seeking the wounded places. In my years of guiding and coaching, I have witnessed that we will only engage this process when we are ready to see. We will only see what is ready to be healed. We are met with what we can handle at every stage of depth work. Ultimately depth process, deepening your own self-knowledge, leads to healing and integration. The honoring of all disowned, neglected, challenging and brilliant parts of self brings them into the whole. This level of self-knowledge serves in unwinding from old patterns, wounds, shadow stories, unconscious beliefs and personal history. Even ancestral wounds and lineage bearing has been healed through parts work.

Many years ago I embarked on a personal journey of deep discovery. I was at a crossroads in my life. Operating through the lens of the "over-thinker" an identified part of self, I favored research and discussion yet I found that many of these old ways were no longer working. I was being called to something new. Vulnerability, insecurity and not knowing surrounded me like a dense fog. I was unsure of how to find and reveal the layers of my authentic self. The task of seeking and uncovering these layers overwhelmed me.

I engaged in a journey of making sense, revealing and unraveling belief as I stripped away my outdated roles and ways of being. This journey required courage and trust, skills I first had to understand, reclaim and then practice until my faith was as robust as my fear.

I sought out my shadow places, discovering the disorganized patterns of my life, moving into mess, creating chaos, sifting and sorting, truth telling and naming. I embraced transformative process and art-making as the language of my soul.

I spent seven years gathering clues that led me back to myself, wandering with purpose, marking my way, sitting in circles, sharing my story, co-creating community and finding my life-work. These spirals led me to a new way of knowing and being; creating a language, a path and a progressive process that gathered my parts back together.

Identifying parts of self was a major influence in reclaiming my life. I first discovered and explored these ideas through my studies of Psychosynthesis and Gestalt Dialoguing and later through shadow and dream work.

Roberto Assagioli founded the psychological movement known as Psychosynthesis. He was an Italian psychiatrist, a pioneer in humanistic and transpersonal psychology who developed many integrative theories. Aligned with Carl Jung's methodologies, Assagioli's model of wholeness included differentiation of conscious states and incorporated humanistic values such as wisdom, creativity and potential. He also was interested in dynamic forms of individuation and development of consciousness that moved one beyond the ordinary.

The organization of sub-personalities is very revealing and sometimes surprising, baffling or even frightening. One discovers how very different and often quite antagonistic traits are displayed in the different roles. These differences of traits, which are organized around a role justify, in our opinion, the use of the word "sub-personality." Ordinary people shift from one to the other without clear awareness, and only a thin thread of memory connects them; but for all practical purposes they are different beings — they act differently, they show very different traits.   *— Roberto Assagioli*

Parts of self are expressed in all directions; they are the good, the bad, and the ugly. They are all aspects of who we have been, who we are and who we will be. They are reflections and expressions of lived, intuited and archetypal experience. Parts of self are living metaphors and symbolic touchstones.

For example, you have been a child. You have been many different kinds of children. Maybe you were one who played in certain ways; maybe you showed up at school with a different sense of ease than you had at home. You might have been a frightened child, a quiet dreamy child, perhaps an adventurous child. Think about how many kinds of children are held within you, their stories and perspective are all there. No longer your lived experience, but are they gone? Or do they continue to be active, residing within you?

Some parts of self are obvious allies. They are light, joy-filled, dynamic and interesting, well understood, appreciated and welcome. Others are more confusing and may leave you feeling unsure, you may even want to slam the door and hide. Some parts of self seem to challenge or frighten.

Shadow is that which cannot be accepted or tolerated, that which is neglected, disowned; in this way even unknown parts of self can carry aspects of our own shadow. When aspects of self present problematic or negative qualities, or expressions, we are often unconscious to our part in these projections. We can look to the things we dislike and find challenging in others to get clear about what we might be projecting. Negative qualities also get projected onto us. When this happens in certain developmental stages, we are vulnerable to believe them; we will perceive them through the lens of our age and experience. We may swallow these "truths" whole and find that they stay with us for years. We carry the seed of an absolute, something bad, not good enough or wrong, which continues to be judged and projected onto, now by ourselves. In this way a false truth can become shadowed and amplified.

Projection, misunderstanding and judgment can activate and amplify our disowned parts over long periods of time. Very often these most shadowed parts and their shadow stories that we hold and carry with us, expressed as hardship, erosion, victim, martyr, roadblocks, sadness, stuckness and grief, are the most powerful places to enter with transformative process. They are also deeply entrenched and finding the entry place to begin working with them, can be challenging.

It is important to make sure you have support. Working with shadow material is powerful energetic work. If you find that you are moving into areas that are triggering, such as past trauma, panic, addiction or extreme reaction, seek the assistance of an advisor, depth coach, medical practitioner, therapist or other appropriate guidance. This kind of energetic depth work is powerful and life changing, at times it needs to be fine-tuned to ones needs and approached with consciousness toward self-care, pacing and guidance.

Everyday offers us a different experience. As individuals we are constantly changing and exploring our parts of self as a way to reflect on the ongoing transitions. Working with parts of self is fluid, not fixed. Gaining new information through revisiting our parts of self is valuable and one of the reasons I recommend integrating imagery and creative process. When working with image and language based forms, one can explore the facets of parts of self by inviting them to speak or show who they are through symbolic language. It is important to remember that every part of self has many facets and details that are holographic, more parts within the whole. There is always an expression of the spectrum, light and darkness, brilliance and challenge, awkwardness and grace. Each part of self is complex and varied, has its own stories, ways of being, distinctive voicing, appearance, history and expression. These may or may not match your exact externalized reflection; rather they are reflective expressions of your whole self, all of the facets, pieces and parts.

Parts of self invite us to explore our life-path finding lost pieces of our own puzzle and bringing them back together to reveal the recognizable image of wholeness. There are many times you may work with a part of self that is not fully revealed, other times you will not be ready to see the nuances that are present. Some of my most shadowed parts have revealed their light sides and evolving nature over long periods of time.

This work can be complex and multi-layered, and is often best approached as extended process. Parts of self are wonderful truth-tellers, revealing our own secrets to us in ways we cannot ignore. Working with them is a powerful way to gather clues, seeking and finding new possibilities within old patterns that are no longer needed.

Threads of stories may be held by and in different parts of self. Stories are patterns of connection and meaning that we develop over a lifetime; story threads are unique reflections of our internal and external life. Parts of self, illuminate our distinctive temperaments, personas and developmental experiences. Through these we create connections and make meaning of what we sense, see, feel, intuit and experience. The word **story** is a container for all the material of life we work with and unpack in transformative process. Using story in this way is a descriptor and does not diminish any content of your life.

From the moment we are able to connect and sense, our lives are filled with experiences or stories. The stories are tied to our parts of self, some are remembered but many more are not. It is our parts of self that bring them back into consciousness. Storied moments in life reflect a full range of emotion and expression, which our parts of self will voice. Stories that are brought to the surface may also be reflective of our known and unknown family, culture, history, community and ancestral connections.

Carl Jung considered that we live within universal archetypal patterns. We can explore these collective patterns through working with parts of self. Working with archetypal energies is another form of self-identification that connects us to our deeper personal myths.

The simplicity and complexity of our parts of self are reflected back to us in everyday life as we work, play and engage with others. When we navigate our fears and follow our needs, wants and desires, we remember these individual aspects and qualities. We are reminded of specific parts of self when walking in nature, looking at the stars and connecting to insights that are intuitive, beyond our thinking mind. We recognize what we are drawn to and resonate with, we remember what we have loved and we tell the truth about what has stripped us to the bone. Through the veil of our own deep history we are reminded of an inner language, the language of image and symbol.

It takes courage to explore in this way. I have embraced parts of self as a method of understanding my deepest identities, traveling into each age, reflection, moment and nuance of my life. I have created space for discovery and witnessing within this unfolding. Recognizing stories that are important and opening to symbolic language, has guided me to identify many parts of self. From this place of gathering I have been able to follow threads of my stories that need to be exposed. The more I know about these hidden truths, the more I know about my whole self.

As Kay Redfield Jameson states,

"Our greatest joys and sorrows ripen on the same vine."

Prompts

What parts of self are identifiable and active?

_____

_____

_____

_____

_____

_____

_____

How do you sense and acknowledge your inner aspects of self?

_____

_____

_____

_____

_____

_____

_____

_____

_____

Which parts of self are stormy and emotional?
Who are they?
What do they look like?
What do they say?

_____

_____

_____

_____

_____

_____

_____

_____

_____

_____

_____

_____

_____

_____

_____

_____

_____

_____

_____

_____

Creative Mapping & Musing

Gathering Wholeness

4 | Ways of Knowing

Gathering wholeness and exploring parts of self is, at its core, consciousness work. Exploring the different levels of consciousness and becoming conscious is part of gathering wholeness. Ways of knowing are varied and fall into six thematic patterns that include Intuitive, Creative, Multiple Perspective, Language & Naming, Life Application (Translation) and Movement. These ways of knowing also interact and combine to create new ways of knowing, unique to each of us.

Wayfinding is a process of identifying one's current path or defining an area of focus, and following it to its source. Utilizing and investigating multiple ways of knowing assists us in engaging exploration as a practice, deepening self-knowledge and activating change.

I consider myself an Artist of Life because I actively utilize and work with these patterns. I believe we are all Artists of Life. Art making is a way of connecting, seeing and engaging. Art is a language of the soul, how it is expressed and used is specific to each individual. Exploring parts of self is a highly creative, ongoing process. It is art making. It is life making.

Intuitive Ways of
Knowing

Personal
Movement

Creative
Process

Life-Path
Application

Multiple
Perspective

Mytho-Poetic
Language &
Naming

Whole Brain/Whole Body

We each have primary operating system. Many of us use a variety of right-brain, left-brain, and embodied sensing/feeling systems to navigate learning styles and creative modalities.

- Some of us are research-based linear thinkers, intellectual seekers at heart.
- Some of us are intuitive learners, gathering symbolic and creative language of art making, dreaming and being states as 'the way in'.
- Some of us are emotional learners, feeling our way through life and gathering clues that swim in and out of our line of sight.
- Some of us are aware of energy states and use our sensing body to filter and understand the world we live in.

As an example, some of us have experienced a lineage, family or community culture that elevated study, research or reliance on information that comes from outside sources; we have a well-developed linear left-brain. On the other hand many of us find that we are shifting to a new way, and may be experiencing a strong pull towards the creative, tangential, non-linear right brain. Do you find that exploring things through trial and error is activating? This new way might trigger a part of self that is unknown, a reflection of creative rising energy. This trial and error process may also activate some memories of getting in trouble for not following rules, activating another part of self that shrinks under the finger of disappointment. These two parts are both reflective of the emerging energy - trial and error. You might also favor a kinesthetic and somatic approach, so the sensation or embodied engagement of trial and error is freeing. Yet another part of self is activated, an incorrigible young trickster who loves to tinker and take things apart. This part of self may be incredibly happy and free in this new state of exploration.

I like to consciously work with the concept of whole brain. Thinking and crossing the hemispheres with a full expression of engaged process utilizes not only the brilliances of the right and left sides of our brain but the potentialities that are imbedded at all levels of consciousness. This whole brain approach is creative by nature because it is non-linear. This concept fits well within gathering wholeness practices and is a way of knowing.

Whole brain must be met with whole body. Like our brain, our body is also incredibly complex. We receive information through our senses, organs and systems; we continue to understand how our bodies are sensitive, intuitive, receptive and generative. This information comes through ways of knowing as well as research based material.

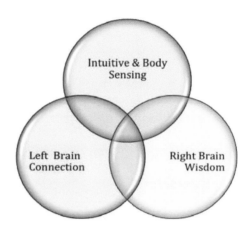

Principles of Gathering Wholeness

Once we turn our attention to the principles of gathering wholeness, we find that the ways and means can guide us:

- **Identify** what is being experienced, felt and sensed using the whole brain, whole body approach.
- **Clarify** what parts of self are shadowed, disowned, misaligned, forgotten or lost.
- **Create** space for seeking and finding with art-making, writing, coaching or transformative process.
- **Gather** all aspects of self, the good, the bad and the ugly. Bring them into your waking consciousness.
- **Deepen** your relationship with the powerful, paradoxical aspects and expressions of self.
- **Expand** your capacity to hold the spectrum of self and experience.
- **Embrace** wholeness as you continue to work with this dynamic material of life.

Creative Process

The creative process itself is a bridge that connects the self to subtle, internal sensing systems. Crossing the bridge and engaging ways of knowing creates a point of access, a connection with the inner landscape of intuition.

Bridging understanding, creating connection and accessing new information are critical parts of any transformative process. Creative and intuitive processes are companions that invite experimentation, another way of bridging the known and unknown territories.

While theories and information systems provide points of reference, they are not more important than the personal, integral, energetic, life affirming and generative power of art and process. Whether exploring parts of self, visual narrative or journey process, art making allows information to be accessed in extraordinary and profound ways.

Options for deepening one's own ways of knowing are extensive. There are many modalities and mediums to explore. These are some that I have found to be particularity powerful:

Our body has a series of complex and complementary **intuitive sensing** systems. Deep within the busy conscious mind are pathways to the interior space of the subconscious mind. Our intuitive sensing can be explored through layers of emotions, feelings, sensations and information held in our whole mind/whole body. Each cell holds the potential for intuitive sensing. We have a powerful intuitive mind in our head and another in our belly, where we feel gut instincts; yet another in our heart where we feel the pull and sensation of love, loss and emotional pain. By connecting to our intuitive senses we create the ability to dive into and understand pools of valuable information, including our shadow stories, wounds and deep desires.

Our ability to **dream and vision**, using the symbolic language as a guide, comes from powerful images we have in our mind's eye. Our dreaming includes various forms such as night dreaming, waking dreams, lucid dreaming, day dreaming and visioning. The symbolic mind reflects image and form that is held within the collective, a base of knowledge that moves through us and operates outside of time. The interior visual images tell the stories of our layers of consciousness and our deeply connected life. Dream work, unpacking dreams and bridging dreams with other depth process is a powerful complementary tool.

Guided and **active imagining** are forms of exploration using visualization, dream work and metaphor to awaken and explore the deep psyche and unconscious mind. The imaginal realm is neither imaginary nor based in our day-to-day experiences, it is rather a vast realm or between space that is fully experienced. The imaginal realm allows us to move into a visual landscape, bringing the dreaming mind to a level of consciousness that can be activated, explored and translated. Other relevant forms of active imagining are engaging psycho-drama and exploring sand tray.

Mytho-poetic **writing, voicing and dialogue** are tools used to identify, language, name and track our journey of self-discovery. These methods are valuable ways to deepen one's own insight and understanding. Through writing, using evocative dialogue, storytelling or poetic style (working with prompts and poetics) we can observe our intuitive thoughts, deep feelings and transformative process, as well as see patterns, repeated symbols, and dream themes. Journaling also stimulates expression of emotions and provides stories of healing.

Indigenous spiritual teachers and healers use **guided and shamanic journeying** to travel and connect to interior or spirit worlds. Realms of spirit animals, ancestors, guides, cosmos and inner realms of the psyche are all common places that hold messages and guidance for the traveler. Using the sound of the voice, drum or rattle, sacred environments are accessed. The traveler may journey to activate healing in the past, present or future, creating a conduit for awareness, healing and movement.

The practice of stilling, quieting and focusing the mind encompass **mindfulness, trance and meditation** techniques. These practices are approached in many ways, and with it a spiritual awareness is often activated. Likewise the creative process can create trance like timeless states, sometimes referred to as being in the zone. Once can also experience connected awareness, increased relaxation and profound insight through mindful movement such as walking the labyrinth, ritual, connecting in nature, yoga and dance. The practice of letting go, clearing the mind and sacred listening will support experiential process.

Creative process is an energetic, **kinesthetic and somatic** process where we use our whole body to explore materials. Art making is embodied movement, the brush is an extension of our body. Energy flows through our hands, through the paint, onto the paper. When we make art we tap into intuitive information and our energy flows and surges in response to the rising energies. There are times one can engage in art-making in such an intense way that strong emotion floods and the body reacts with exhaustion, illness and pain. Care must be taken to meet one's own physical needs when creating in this way. Art as movement can be explored through chi gong, yoga, conscious dance; all ways to release tension and invite flow.

Many forms of expressive and transformative art, value **art as process**. Exploring forms that are accessible, enjoyable, engaging in what is happening in the making process itself rather than focusing on the product; releases a tendency to dwell on technique, perfectionism and outcome. Materials and process include Collage, Mixed Media, Found Art, Assemblage, Process Painting, Maskmaking, Drawing, Art Journaling, Altered Books, Photography, Altar Building, Doll Arts, Visual Narrative, Storytelling and Poetics. Specific forms such as *Mythos Journey*, SoulCollage® and Touch Drawing can be very powerful ways to connect self-knowledge to a structured form.

Prompts

What is a **way of knowing** that feels potent and active?

_____

_____

_____

_____

_____

_____

Which creative process seems the most relevant and engaging to you right now?

_____

_____

_____

_____

_____

_____

_____

How do you embrace and find value in intuitive and non-linear experience?

_____

_____

_____

_____

_____

_____

_____

_____

What is inspiring your art, writing and process techniques?

_____

_____

_____

_____

_____

_____

_____

_____

_____

_____

_____

Creative Mapping & Musing

Gathering Wholeness

5 | Tracking Perspective

Gathering our parts, seeking clarity, re-aligning and finding balance are all reasons we work with wholeness. In order to effectively work with parts of self we must be able to explore and look at ourselves from multiple perspectives. What looks like a flat circle from one angle becomes a three-dimensional sphere when seen from another point of view; creating new vantage points can be challenging and have surprising value in depth process. Tracking the movement and exploring the resulting information can be marked in many ways. This can include using repeated images, symbols, words or working through layers, themes and iterations.

Much like walking on a path and leaving stones in a specific stacked pattern, we can mark our passage as we navigate between parts of self or move beyond the edges of our original map. Gaining new perspective and expanding our points of view stretch our edges, expanding and shifting what we know to be true. That in turn increases our range of motion as we translate transformative process, into a transformed life.

Look at the image below…

Are you comfortable with this image?

What do you feel in your body when you see it?

Ok, Now how does this image feel?

BE NOWHERE

How does this image speak to you now?

Do you notice any emotions emerging?

Do you notice any emotions surfacing?

How does this image change you?

BE HERE NOW

How does this feel different?

How do these words impact you?

How do these words inspire you?

The same letters make up each of these phrases.

What about this **multiple perspective exercise** might be reflective of your working with your own Parts of Self?

BE HERE NOW

BE NO WHERE

Finding Clues in Strange Places

Be Here Now and Be No Where, is something I discovered through a piece of art. Random word charms, on the ends of wire rearranged themselves to show me this word play.

Something happened in that moment; a deep insight was activated, a doorway opened inside. Possibility was expanded with dynamic perspective.

- Where are your clues?
- What do they look like and where are they hidden?
- Do you explore image, color and texture as a language of emotion or movement?
- What symbols show up frequently in your space and life?
- Are your feelings reflected through seasons, weather or elements?

Perspectives & Healing Art

Much of my early professional work was focused on stigma, shame and healing, particularly within emotional states and deep wounds. Several years later after I had shifted focus, I was following clues and paying attention when I came up with the idea of creating a blanket out of book pages. This was not to be any ordinary quilt, it was a Blanket of Shame and I choose to use a very old family book of Aesop's Fables. I particularly disliked this book as a child. For many, this is a beloved book, and yet I was following a thread and choose to trust my own inner instincts.

I felt in my core that it was a shaming book, representing punitive patriarchy. I gave myself permission to ruin and deconstruct it, to make something new with it. This was only possible for me to do without activating 'the good girl' because I had unraveled my own shame deeply enough, to be able to activate and explore multiple perspectives within the making process. A hand stitched healing scroll initially inspired the quilted form.

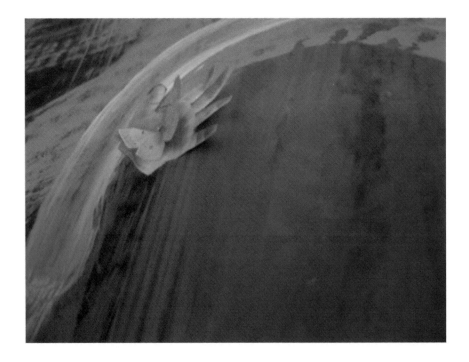

I was specifically focused on shame that was the residue of pain perpetrated against children. Although this was not my personal experience as a child, I was channeling something that I felt deeply connected to. I had a whole story running about what I was feeling and it seemed to direct itself toward active healing on behalf of collective male shame, boy shame. The cycles of shame, neglect, abuse and pain is generational, non-discriminant and pervasive. I worked in social services settings for many years and was faced with the resulting outcomes of neglect and abuse on boys and girls, impacting men and women of all ages.

I came to know that I was exploring what was written between the lines. It was not just the book pages, not just the surface moral tales, but I was concerned with the underlying collective seeds of shame. This Blanket of Shame became a personal meditation in healing the collective. Book pages stitched together like a quilt, sized to fit a small mattress. I used my own baby blankets from infancy, the ones that traveled with me from foster placements to my adoptive home, I hid them underneath the blanket of shame. These also represented to me the complex paradoxical state of love and shame co-existing.

It became an installation piece, a poignant reflection of my sense of subtle shame. It was a reminder of historical shame being inflicted on children in their beds by their parents in quiet and effective ways. As I created this piece I was aware of my own mistakes as a parent. I thought about the pain I felt when my children were ill treated and misunderstood. I remember moments of my misplaced anger lashing out in wrong directions. Memory threads of my small son, who was shamed by his teacher for playful exuberance, lost his trust of all teachers.

I stitched my pain and sorrow into the quilt as I considered the residual effect of subtle and systematic wounding perpetuated within families, communities and society at large. I wrote messages of healing and reconciliation in between the lines and sent my intention into the world. The Blanket of Shame evolved over time and ultimately held the energy of healing that I had intended. Later it was incorporated into a traveling apothecary that represented restorative journeys and healing stories.

Prompts

How do you see your Self(s) from multiple perspectives?

_____

_____

_____

_____

_____

_____

_____

_____

_____

Invite creative expression to guide your exploration and offer you different vantage points.

_____

_____

_____

_____

_____

_____

_____

Gather images that pull you in, or art that you have previously created, and notice what parts of self you see and recognize:

_____

_____

_____

_____

_____

_____

_____

_____

_____

_____

_____

_____

Creative Mapping & Musing

Explore your edges
Make space

Be Here Now

The wild
dance
with life
pulls
at your
spirit.

Stop
Float
Listen

Who am I

to be

come

Ebb and flow.
the tides will carry you.

Let them
return you
to your

whole self.

      - Cat Caracelo

6 | Cycles & Phases

Working with cycles and phases of life, our own or those that are experienced, observed or held within the collective, can be a powerful point of entry toward gathering wholeness. We meet ourselves reflected in image and form. Channeling lived and intuited memory we journey within many life cycles and archetypal phases. Each of these represents our own experience of those ages and stages. These references are often brought into focus as parallel memory threads meeting one another, in life. Often memories and reference points meet us in ways we cannot ignore.

We are not only who we are now, but also who we have ever been, and who we will be. These multi-level experiences are held within our body and become expressed in myriad ways through our parts of self.

Memory is a shifting and illusive thing.

Exploring or unpacking the nuances of each part of self, what you experienced and felt at any pivotal moment of your life is filtered through the lens of that particular developmental age. Applying a variety of perspectives or cross pollinating your self-knowledge with ideas, distinctions, details and theoretical information can be a dynamic way to reflect the diversity embedded within our parts, stories and expressions of self.

This offers some dynamic ways of working with and applying multiple expressions. We are always gathering wholeness even when it feels like we are deep in the depths of old stories and deep pain. The potential for clarity and expansion is activated when there is a conscious connection made to cycles of life and ages and stages. It is an important part of depth work and extended process. I invite you to work with these ideas in a curious, experiential and exploratory way.

"Be patient toward all that is unsolved in your heart and try to love the questions themselves, like locked rooms and like books that are now written in a very foreign tongue. Do not now seek the answers, which cannot be given you because you would not be able to live them. And the point is, to live everything. Live the questions now. Perhaps you will then gradually, without noticing it, live along some day into the answer"
— Ranier Maria Rilke

Years ago within a guided journey experience, I was surprised to find a small, emaciated and dirty vampire child. She was dwelling deep in an underground grotto; she was sad and fearful, emitting energetic waves of deep mistrust. She was not frightening or pathetic, although I was aware that others might have seen that in her; rather, I felt in my own body her sense of profound overwhelm. It was a kind of flooding horror. Through her, this one single part of self that I had no conscious knowledge of, I began to journey and unravel my own history of being connected to feeling states, being overwhelmed by the emotional pain of others and blocking my own expression of strong emotion. I gathered and worked with memory threads of my earliest sense of being flooded by emotional pain. I painted, made collages, and wrote as I explored these experiences. I explored my womb time, when I was in utero and my birth mother was planning my adoption. I re-remembered a time later in my infancy after she decided to keep me, her sadness and confusion permeated my small psychic space and I put on armor to protect myself. I found places of deep sorrow and crystalline clarity, understanding how I had developed many parts of self, very early in my life, to navigate some of these pre-verbal experiences. I explored this through many mediums, making art, dreaming, moving, writing and visioning. Through this one opening, I activated my own healing, developed new abilities and strengthened my boundaries. My vampire child was a doorway to discovery and illumination.

Carl Jung shares, *"Your vision becomes clear when you look inside your own heart, who looks outside dreams, who looks inside, awakes."* He speaks of exploring the shadows of the self, the dark places that seem frightening. It is often in these places that we find information that is the exact light and illumination we are seeking.

Early in my career, as an undergraduate psychology student, I began to develop a theory of individuation. At that time most of my research and experience was guiding me toward studies in reducing shame and stigma, focusing on cultivating resilience and developmental capacity to change. I was exploring the distinctive points of integration within one's developmental ages and stages, the first I believe occurring at the time of entering. There are many points of integration that occur throughout childhood and into late adult years. These points of integration support one's sense of wholeness and can also impact the opposite, a sense of being fractured, fragmented or broken that I refer to as disintegration.

Psycho-spiritually a state of disintegration is a place of learning and growth, but it often feels challenging and can be perceived as impending death. It is in fact a kind of death, in preparation for something new; things fall apart. We cycle through periods of natural integration and disintegration, but these natural cycles may be interrupted by adverse circumstances, trauma and perception through the lens of one's developmental challenges. Many things challenge development including temperament, circumstances, misunderstandings, learning differences and sensitivities to name a few. We wonder how one child thrives in a family and another withers. We notice how we never fit, were not seen or heard or honored for special qualities and gifts, as a child. These are points of pain that can stall integration.

As one seeks higher states of individuation and wholeness, these missed points of integration may need to be returned to, reactivated in some way, to find the source of pain and activate healing. The facets and complexities of self, expressions, identities, cause and effect, parallel pathways and periods of disintegration can be healed. Choosing to engage process, being conscious and mapping the connections, will assist in healing.

There is no timeline for how we experience the affect of pain held in our developmental ages and stages. In the blink of an eye we are triggered and find our self in reaction. Unpleasant reactive behaviors from one of our young selves, is activated and we are left with a mess; shame gets piled on top of shame. When we can pinpoint, remember or are drawn back into moments in time; we can process and then heal. Integration of our undigested 'material of life' is a symbiotic process, utilizing the rhythms of integration and disintegration. We must find accessible ways to work with our own points of pain, confusion and loss, in order to activate movement.

Comparative Theories

There are many theories that help us to explore our own ages and stages.

Erik Erikson, a developmental psychologist offers an extensive multi-perspective theory that outlines points of integration and disintegration; including details that illuminate one's own parts of self that may not be fully remembered. These nuances invite us to explore stages, such as pre-verbal or early childhood. These helps us recognize hidden, lost and disowned parts of self.

I have overlaid my Intuitive/Feminine Phases of Development, as a way to identify and language deep and resonate experiences that are relevant to a larger intuitive feminine paradigm of wholeness. The additional references to archetypal patterns are another way of providing information and cross-comparison. This form of integrating multiple models is extremely valuable when exploring parts of self. We learn things about who are when we can explore ideas through multiple lenses and languages. Theories and patterns provide multiples lenses, as do images and symbols.

Looking over the comparative model, notice how the different language may draw you in. This is an easy way to access a lot of information and find the things that speak directly to you. Look at this information using the whole brain/whole body approach. Feel you way through it and find the details that remind you of something you need to know. Create with those things and expand on them. Trust you ways of knowing.

Gathering Wholeness | Identifying and Working with Parts of Self
Comparative Psycho-Spiritual Developmental Ages and Stages © Cat Caracelo M.A.

Stage/Age	Erikson's Basic Developmental Conflict	Caracelo's Intuitive/Feminine Phases of Development (Archetypal Reference)	Important Events	Erikson's Developmental Outcome
Birth - 18 Months	Trust vs. Mistrust	Womb Time (Spirit) Birth /Entering (Infant)	Feeding	Children develop a sense of trust when caregivers provide reliability, care, and affection. A lack of this will lead to mistrust.
2 to 3 years old	Autonomy vs. Shame and Doubt	Finding Breath & Voice Learning Trust & Touch Dreaming & Memory Keeping Nature of Temperament (Child)	Toilet Training	Children need to develop a sense of personal control over physical skills and a sense of independence. Success leads to feelings of autonomy, failure results in feelings of shame and doubt.
3 to 5	Initiative vs. Guilt	Nature of Resiliency Patterns of Play Age of Claiming & Shaming Emotional Literacy Bridging Imaginal/ Literal Realms	Exploration	Children need to begin asserting control and power over the environment. Success in this stage leads to a sense of purpose. Children who try to exert too much power experience disapproval, resulting in a sense of guilt.
6 to 11	Industry vs. Inferiority	Age of Separating Threshold Years	School	Children need to cope with new social and academic demands. Success leads to a sense of competence, while failure results in feelings of inferiority.
12 to 20	Identity vs. Role Confusion	Age of Body (Maiden) Expansion/Contraction Blooming Opening and Activating Identity Explored	Social Relationships	Teens needs to develop a sense of self and personal identity. Success leads to an ability to stay true to ones self, while failure leads to role confusion and a weak or challenging sense of self.
21-28	Intimacy vs. Isolation	Age of Exploration Connecting into World & Others Extending Self with Care Mothering (Mother)	Relationships	Young adults need to form intimate, loving relationships with other people. Success leads to strong relationships, while failure often results in loneliness and isolation.
28-35	Generatively vs. Stagnation	Age of Competency Skill Building		

www.catcaracelo.com

Gathering Wholeness | Identifying and Working with Parts of Self
Comparative Psycho-Spiritual Developmental Ages and Stages © Cat Caracelo M.A.

35-42	Generatively vs. Stagnation	**Age of Seeking** **Identifying Lack/Grief/Fear** **Emotional Literacy**	Work and Parenthood	Adults need to create or nurture things that will outlast them, often by having children or creating a positive change that benefits other people. Success leads to feelings of usefulness and accomplishment, while failure results in shallow involvement in the world.
42-49		**Age of Ritual Time/Reconnecting** **Early Re-Claiming**		
49-56		**Early Wisdom-Gathering (Crone),** **Age of Healing** **Reconnecting Body/Mind/Spirit** **Moving into the Deep Realms** **Exploring/Integrating Shadow** **Claiming Creative Ways** **Choice and Voice**		
56-63		**Age of Translation** **Redefining Self & Purpose**	Reflection on Life	Older adults need to look back on life and feel a sense of fulfillment. Success at this stage leads to feelings of wisdom, while failure results in regret, bitterness, and despair. **Intuitive Phases: Often a time of complexity, re-evaluation and transitioning. Recasting of definitions of worth, productivity, wellness and wholeness.** Maslow's Level of Self-Actualization: Morality, Creativity, Spontaneity, Lack of prejudice, Problem solving, Acceptance of facts.
63-70	Ego Integrity vs. Despair	**Age of Deep Listening** **Recasting Meaning/Value** **Amplified Choice and Voice**		
70-77		**Energetic Realignment** **Unraveling and Reweaving**		
77-84		**Connecting with Between** **Traveling through the Veil/Mist** **Seeking and Finding Wisdom**		
84-91		**Unraveling and Re-weaving** **Sifting and Sorting** **Recasting Meaning and Value** **Placement**		
91-98		**Age of Touching** **Exploring Dreamtime & Spirit** **Gathering & Releasing** **Gratitude**		
98-106		**Age of Releasing Breath**		
106+		**Age of Spirit**		

www.catcaracelo.com

Symbolic Phases & The Moon

Another interesting and equally evocative way to work with this material is to look at phases and cycles of life through the symbolic reference of the moon.
The Moon is an ancient symbol of reflection, expressing the embodiment of divine feminine and receptive energies in all of their expressions regardless of gender identity.

Symbolically aligned with emotions, intuition and illuminating darkness the moon offers different faces and expressions in each of her phases. The moon reminds us of powerful symbolic patterns and cycles that guide us differently. These are some facets of moon lore that may spark your own connection with your phases of life:

- Many cultures marked the start of their new day at moonrise.
- Women have created connection and ritual, aligning blood cycles and birthing rituals with moon time.
- The moon's gravitational pull causes the tides to shift.
- Planting by the cycles of the moon is an ancient system known in every culture.
- The moon travels the night sky in different trajectories according to the seasons, at times hanging low in the sky just above the horizon and other times arching a path high into the starry sky.

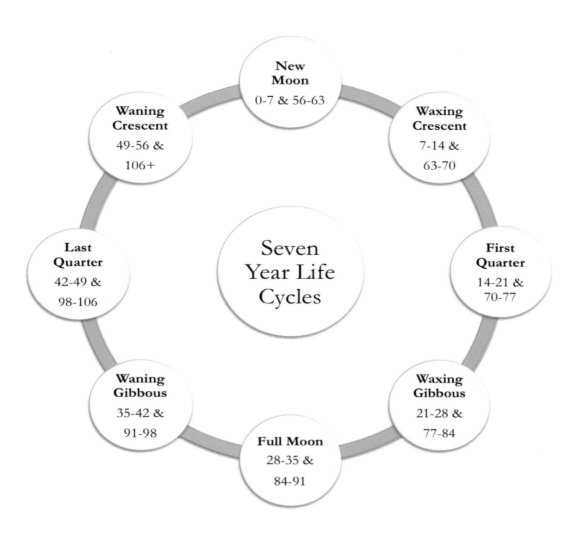

The phases from New Moon to Full Moon are called the Waxing Moon. Full Moon to New Moon time is called the Waning Moon.

New Moon
The new moon is connected with initiation, increased consciousness, focusing the emotions and vision.

Waxing Moon
As the fullness of the moon increases, the brightening reflects a time of strengthening the emotional and spiritual forces that promote growth and prosperity. This is the moon time of wicking and sap rising.

Full Moon

The fullness of the moon represents full light and open reflection, marking completion, wholeness, abundance and flowing generosity.

Waning Moon

The moon is decreasing in fullness, moving into the darkness. This is the time of the darkening, a time that corresponds with energetic resting and renewal.

The moon phases may be applied to our own life cycles, as reflected in the matrix, yet we can also apply the phases of the moon to seven-year life cycles, or other multi year phases that are relevant for you. In this way we are activating a form of pattern play that re-orients our perspective. In this model we may see new connections are important demarcations of our own patterns of ebb and flow, integration and disintegration, growth and renewal.

Prompts

What age or memory thread of a particular life stage, calls to you for deeper exploration?

_____

_____

_____

_____

_____

_____

_____

Where are you in your own life cycle right now? Is there a feeling of integration or disintegration at this time of your life?

_____

_____

_____

_____

_____

_____

_____

_____

What parts of self are emerging, or seem very active?
How many parts are present?
Are they oppositional or paradoxical?
What is being activated by their presence?

_____

_____

_____

_____

_____

_____

_____

_____

_____

_____

_____

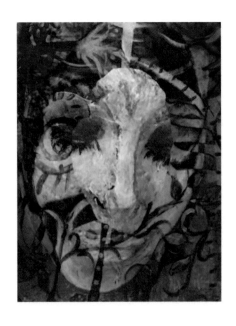

Creative Mapping & Musing

7 | Traveling the Spectrum

Exploring parts of self within a spectrum model will serve to deepen your connection with your known and unknown stories, healing patterns of the past and claiming aspects of self that are emerging.

The spectrum points to the multiplicity and complexity of who we are:

WHO ARE YOU?

WHO ARE YOU, NOW?

These are very two simple yet powerful questions and the answers that are held within them will illustrate new truths <u>each time</u> they are answered. Every aspect, piece and part of self whether expressed internally or externally, found in the past, the present or the future, has this same complexity. The spectrum if applied as a model of any whole, is relative to that which is present. So in this way wholeness can be applied to small details, states of being, forms of movement, energies, parts of self and stuff of life, as well as larger constructs.

The *Spectrum of Self* is reflective of the many facets of our human experience, held within our various roles and personae. They include the intuited parts of self, elements of life-stages and archetypal patterns we have lived or recognize within our self and others. The spectrum of self will include aspects of shadow and light, values, that which we honor and accept, and also that which we abhor and reject.

The *Spectrum of Experience* is the range of remembered, felt, perceived, interpreted and envisioned experience. Experiences may encompass deep history, ancestral awareness, the unconscious collective, one's own past, present and future.
Exploring societal and familial value placement, messages that lead to shame, perceptions of pain, fear, sadness and confusion, which are often influenced by the lens of developmental age, understanding, vulnerability, temperament and resilience, are important avenues of inquiry.

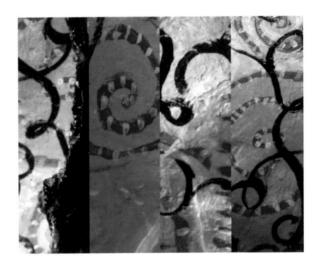

I had been developing and working with the *Spectrum of Self* and *Spectrum of Experience* models for many years when I heard Jungian analyst Marian Woodman speak on the topic of holding the tension of opposites. Woodman shared that the tension that is held within paradox or opposition can be felt and explored as the energetics of disease. Yet I have come to understand that the tension of opposites may also be a well-formed habit and a pattern of conscious or unconscious belief that can be explored and worked with, in order to invite release. When viewed through multiple perspectives, tension may ease and become newly perceived as traveling.

Working within a form or structure journey of discovery, the tightness of tension can shift to traveling, and we may find our self in a place of curiosity and wonder. Through extended process we can identify and give voice to parts of self, and more complex connections and patterns. As we journey with these facets of our self, we explore our own depths, creating connections, deepening understanding and activating healing.

Exploring the *Spectrum of Self* requires a safe place to unfold our truths; the practice often inspires newfound connections. Spectrum work is about deepening our self-knowledge; it takes courage to explore in this way. I have embraced transformative arts as a method of truth telling, exploring my deepest true self, in each age, reflection, moment and nuance of life.

The *Spectrum of Self* is the full reflection of the many aspects of human-ness that impact us as individuals, including sensation, feeling, expression and mood. The good, the bad and the ugly, that is experienced both internally and externally, is the human experience. The miraculous, the mischievous, the funky, the amazing, the funny, the painful, playful and edgy parts of self are able to be discovered, seen and worked with; allowed and expressed more deeply within art process.

As I have shared before, there is amazing insight and wisdom found in exploring the shadow material one's own life. The disowned and ignored parts of self, generational pain, ancestral and collective shadow, often become swallowed by the self and semi-forgotten. The experiences trouble our inner waters.

This construct, bringing together parts of self and spectrum work, can reveal important information that assists in clarifying and evolving your life experience. When you understand the pattern that is being held within a single spectrum you also hold the knowledge of choice and voice. You can ask as series of powerful questions to create new movement.

Using your favorite ways and means, including art, words, voicing or other reflective tools, ask yourself: What spectrum is calling my attention?

 Who is active on each end of the spectrum?

 Who is living in the spectrum between?

- What does this spectrum look like?
- What are the images or touchstones that you see?
- What do you feel and recognize through other senses?
- Notice how you are holding your body.
- If you are using images reflect on embodied posture and stance.
- Feel the contours of your face, as you speak words that are bubbling up through the surface of this spectrum.
- Feel the emotions that are present.

The information held within the spectrum is multi directional; it can be delved into, excavated and mined, it can be expanded on and grown in new directions.
One may find resistance, challenge and disorientation when engaging depth process. Tiredness, reluctance and discomfort are always powerful clues that one has tapped into a hot topic. Resistance to go deeper is always fear, although it will show up in other forms. The fear that the deeper we go the hotter it will be, activates inner warning systems, like "Not Safe".

Think of the volcanic activity under the crust of the earth. These sources of energy are the material of life, dynamic, energetic and explosive in nature. Tapping into vents, releasing steam and allowing the flow space to direct itself, is exactly how new growth is created and how energy is produced. Stay with it, make space for a long process where you are energetically expanding your edges, activating and traveling in new, expansive territory. Allow yourself time to be with these ideas and ease them into consciousness.

There is enormous power in naming and identifying parts of self, and the spectrum can make this process even more useful. Compare and contrast what is active; identifying information using words, names, writing and dialoguing, taps into vital information that you might not know otherwise.

You might find that you are working with an overactive anxiety and you identify a part of self that you call the Anxious One. You probably know what that part looks like, how old he or she is, how their voice is toned, which distinctive energies and movement mark the passage of this Anxious One. You actually might think you are exploring movement because the inner quality of anxiety is so uncomfortable; maybe you work with spectrum of self and activate a reflection of another part called the Creative Dancer. You work with this part exploring all of the ways this is active and dynamically different. Where one jerks and starts, the other flows and interacts with grace and ease. They will likely inform and influence your life in very different ways.

What if they are on the same spectrum? And the Spectrum is called TRUST. How might this spectrum also hold other parts? What other memory threads are connected to trust and lack of trust?

Consider how many expressions of trust might need to be explored, where they enter into the spectrum and how these parts of self interact together. Many parts can be held and explored within the spectrum.

The thinking mind is a great meaning maker; the thinking mind wants to get stuck in old ways, where there is comfort and safety. If resistance is present, bring it in to the spectrum. If the critic is present, work with it in the spectrum. If you find that there is a family tree full of challengers and doubters, invite them to become known by bringing the whole group into the spectrum.

Dialoguing with Parts

Many forms of dialoguing are useful to open up the 'voice' of our parts of self. When we invite the voicing to be expressed through us, written or verbal, we hear our self in new ways. There are many forms and techniques of voicing, several that work well with parts work.

A classic Psychosynthesis and SoulCollage® Voicing is:
I am the one who…
What I have to say to you is…
My gift to you is…

Intuitive Storytelling as Voicing:
Using third person or object to begin a story.
She wandered in the darkness……

The branches hung low and the owl blinked...

Path/Map Voicing:
I am the way of...
I am the place of...
I am guiding you by...
I challenge you with...
What I have to tell you is...

Discovery Voicing:
I am the:
My feeling/emotion is:
My landscape is:
My experience is:
My season is:
My need is:
I sense:

Shadow/Challenger Voicing:
I am the face of...
I am the one who reveals...
I live in the wound of...
My purpose is...
I am an ally/ a challenger/ both

Prompts for Mapping and Marking Place:
This is the heart of...
The energy that dwells here is...
I notice...
The season is...
The time of day tells me...
The elements that surround me are...
Under this place there dwells...
Beyond the veil...

Prompts

Where are you experiencing and holding tension?

_____

_____

_____

_____

_____

_____

_____

_____

_____

_____

What parts of self seem to be connected in unusual ways?

_____

_____

_____

_____

_____

_____

_____

_____

_____

What is emerging? Is there a part of self that is being birthed?

_____

_____

_____

_____

_____

_____

_____

_____

_____

_____

_____

Creative Mapping & Musing

Gathering Wholeness

8 | Gathering Wholeness

We live in many directions. Throughout our lifetime we experience joy, sorrow, lessons and learning. We traverse myriad developmental stages, in and out of chronological time. We navigate our way through circumstance, pain and challenge. We are expressed internally and externally, as one and as many. We are living contradictions, held between paradoxes. Yet, within our many parts, we find reflections of our own wholeness.

"We live in a house of mirrors and think we are looking out the windows"
-Fritz Perls

Gathering Wholeness is deep and powerful work. It happens over a lifetime. It is self directed for the most part, birthed through sacred listening, answering the call to heal and embracing dynamic personal practice.

Deepening the work and extending the process is a way to reestablish the strong connective tissues that are necessary for our wholeness. The cycles of disintegration that we experience feel like dismemberment. Alternatively, cycles of integration are rememberment. We are literally remembering how to listen when we hear the call and turn our attention to working with parts of self.

We may cycle through periods of integration and disintegration over our lifetime, but when we have activated and developed process and practice, healed wounded places, and have found lost parts; we cannot return to the same wholly dismembered state again. Connective tissues allow our joints to be stable, rotate and move with ease. It is the fascia and muscle that gives our bodies structural strength; binding areas together where we need support while providing suppleness and range of motion where we need flexibility and flow.

Clarissa Pinkola Estes shares about the woman who sings over the bones, in her book *Women Who Run With the Wolves*. This story speaks to the deep need we have, to recover our lost parts. In the story, singing is the ritual practice that is activated from deep within the whole self, used to energetically call her parts back home.

A keening or wail of our deep sorrows may be present as we realize we are in a state of dismemberment or disintegration. We may be stunned and confused, or numb and tired, realizing that we have been drifting for some time. We hear a call and find ourselves awakening. We find voice through process and practice, gathering the energy that is required to face our dismemberment. This becomes the active force that allows for rememberment, the opposite energy of dismemberment. Active remembering, like the song that is sung over the bones, brings our parts back into the whole.

This voicing is a happening, a choice to tell the truth about our scattered parts. This is an activation of movement, flow and expression.

Grief, loss and confusion may be present in states of disintegration, but connecting and taking action moves energies that have been stuck and unexpressed. As we gather our parts and create structural support, in ways that are deeply meaningful to us, we strengthen our connective tissue. We discover that we are activating deep healing, as we with our parts and integrate them into the whole. We also find over time, that our extended practice is creating movement in new directions and growing our capacity .

Developing a personal symbolic language that will illuminate the unfolding process of gathering wholeness is necessary. Simply rushing through process to experience outcomes is not going to activate deep healing. The personal language, which might be an art form or process, is foundational when working with more complex personal mythos, archetypal connections and extended journey process. Understanding the interconnected web of ones own life stories, working deeply with parts of self, ways of knowing, multi-faceted perspective, cycles, developmental ages and stages, symbolic and archetypal phases, shadow and spectrum, is life altering.

This style of depth work and process brings one into relationship with a new way of being. It is activated with energy, healing and relationship building that is experienced from the inside out. Gathering wholeness works like the tides, becoming regular and rhythmic. As one gets used to the rhythm of this work, ebbing and flowing through day-to-day life, there will be an effect of calming, a consistency that is based in trusting the whole self.

Gathering wholeness also has a strong ripple effect, and tides can rise as energy creates sea change. Transformative change is never held inside for long, it must be shared through the self, into the world. Self-knowledge expands the spectrum of self, then the spectrum of self becomes new experience, new experience translates into choice and voice and the integrative facets of wholeness expand in all directions.

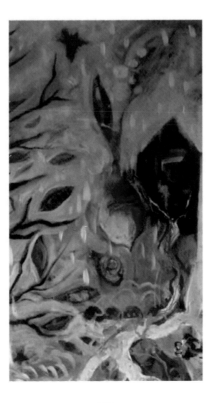

References

Allen, P. (1995) *Art is a Way of Knowing*. Boston: Shambhala Publications.

Allen, P. (2005) *Art is Spiritual Path*. Boston: Shambhala Publications.

Arrien, A., (1987) *The Tarot Handbook, Practical Applications of Ancient Visual Symbols*. New York: Jeremy P Tarcher/Putnam

Arrien, A., (2005) *The Second Half of Life*. Colorado: Sounds True.

Bache, C. (2008) *The Living Classroom: Teaching and Collective Conscious*. New York: State of University of New York Press.

Bierlein, J. (1994) *Parallel Myths*. New York: Random House.

Bolen, J. (1994) *Crossing to Avalon*. San Francisco: HarperCollins.

Bolen, J. (1996) *Close to the Bone*. San Francisco: Conari Press.

Bolen, J. (1984) *Goddesses in Everywoman*. San Francisco: HarperCollins.

Brody, H. (1982) *Maps and Dreams*. New York: Random House.

Chalquist, C., Elliott, R. (2009) *Storied Lives, Discovering and Deepening Your Personal Myth*. Walnut Creek: World Soul Books

Colorado, A. (1995). *Remembrance: An intercultural mental health process*. First Reading. Vol 13:3.

Erikson, E. H.. (1959) *Identity and the Life Cycle. Selected Papers*. New York. International Universities Press.

Estes, C. (1995) *Women Who Run with the Wolves, Myths and Stories of the Wild Woman Archetype*. New York: Ballantine Books.

Ford, D. (1998) *The Dark Side of the Light Chasers*. New York: Riverhead Books

Gallegos, E. (1987) *The Personal Totem Pole, Animal Imagery, the Chakras and Psychotherapy*. New Mexico: New Moon Press

Goleman, D. (1995) *Emotional Intelligence*. New York: Bantam Books.

Gould, J. (2005) *Spinning Straw into Gold, What Fairytales Reveal about the Transformations in a Woman's Life*. New York: Random House.

Houston, J. (1996) *A Mythic Life, Learning to Live our Greater Story*. San Francisco: Harper Collins.

Jaenke, K. (2000) *Personal Dreamscape as Ancestral Landscape.* Unpublished PhD
    Dissertation, California Institute of Integral Studies.

Jung, C., Hull, R. (1971) *The Portable Jung.* New York: Viking Press

Light, C., (1996) *The Way of the Doll, The Art and Craft of Personal Transformation.*
    San Francisco: Chronicle Books

Markova, D. (1994) *No Enemies Within.* Berkeley: Conari Press.

Moore, T. (2004) *Dark Nights of the Soul.* New York: Gotham Books

Perls, F. (1973) *The Gestalt Approach & Eye Witness to Therapy.* New York, NY: Bantam
Books.

Richo, D. (1999) *Shadow Dance, Liberating the Power and Creativity of your Dark Side.*
    Boston: Shambhala.

Samuels, M., Lane, M. (1998) *Creative Healing, How to Heal Yourself by Tapping your
    Hidden Creativity.* San Francisco: HarperCollins.

Samuels, M., Lane, M. (2000) *Spirit-Body Healing: Using Your Mind's Eye to Unlock the
    Medicine Within.* New York: Wiley; 2000.

Simpkinson, C., Simpkinson, A., ed. (1993) *Sacred Stories: A Celebration of the Power of
Story to Transform and Heal.* San Francisco: Harper Collins.

Strickling, B. (2007) *Dreaming about the Divine.* New York: State University of New
York Press.

Walker, B. (1985) *The Crone.* San Francisco: Harper Collins.

Walker, B. (1988) *The Woman's Dictionary of Symbols and Sacred Objects.* San Francisco:
    Harper Collins.

Zweig, C., Abrams J. (1991) *Meeting the Shadow.* New York: Jeremy P Tarcher/Putnam
Books